Playing with Solar Heat

Published in the United States of America by Cherry Lake Publishing
Ann Arbor, Michigan
www.cherrylakepublishing.com

Reading Adviser: Marla Conn MS, Ed., Literacy specialist, Read-Ability, Inc.
Book Design: Jennifer Wahi
Illustrator: Jeff Bane

CIP data has been filed and is available at catalog.loc.gov

Printed in the United States of America
Corporate Graphics Inc.

About the illustrator: Jeff Bane and his two business partners own a studio along the American River in Folsom, California, home of the 1849 Gold Rush. When Jeff's not sketching or illustrating for clients, he's either swimming or kayaking in the river to relax.

table of contents

Science Notes

Playing with Solar Heat explores the basics of solar heat. In this experiment, the reader leaves 3 different colored bottles out in the sun. Results will show that the black bottle will be the warmest while the white one is the coolest. This demonstrates how dark colors absorb heat and light colors reflect heat.

The sun is hot. It gives off **solar** heat. It keeps the earth warm.

What other facts do you
know about the sun?

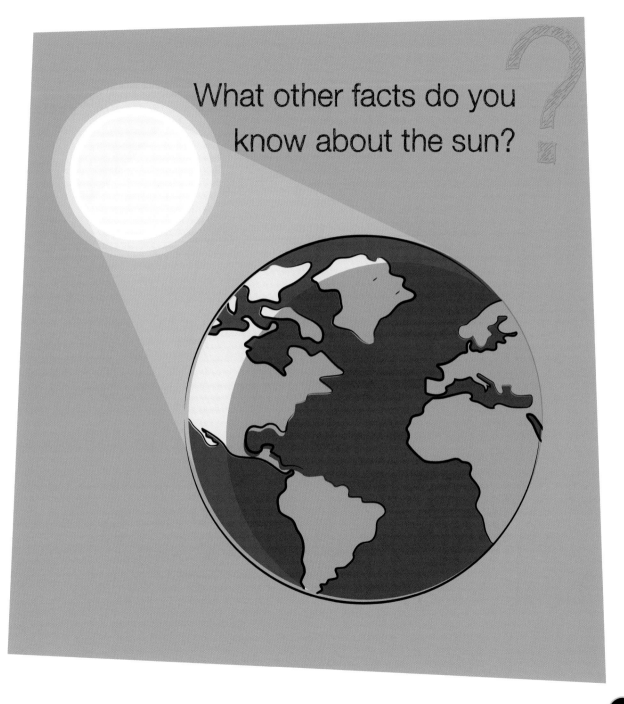

Can you control where solar heat goes?

Let's find out!

We will try to measure heat using bottles of water.

- 3 clear plastic water bottles

- White paint

- Black paint

- Outdoor deck or **windowsill**

You will need
these things

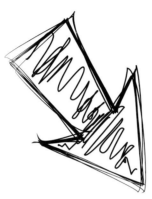

BLACK

WHITE

Paint one bottle white. Paint another black. Leave the other one plain.

What do you think the paint will do?

Put water in the bottles. On a sunny day, put them outside.

After a few hours, bring the bottles inside. Touch them. Pour the water on your hands. Notice how warm it is. Which one feels warmest?

The black bottle will be warmest. The white bottle will be coolest. Why do you think this is?

Try this with jars instead of bottles. Try it with ice instead of water. Try it on a cloudy day. What happens?

Good job. You're done!
Science is fun!

What new questions do you have?

glossary

solar (SOH-lur) having to do with the sun

windowsill (WIN-doh-sil) the ledge at the bottom of a window

index